LOVING VENICE

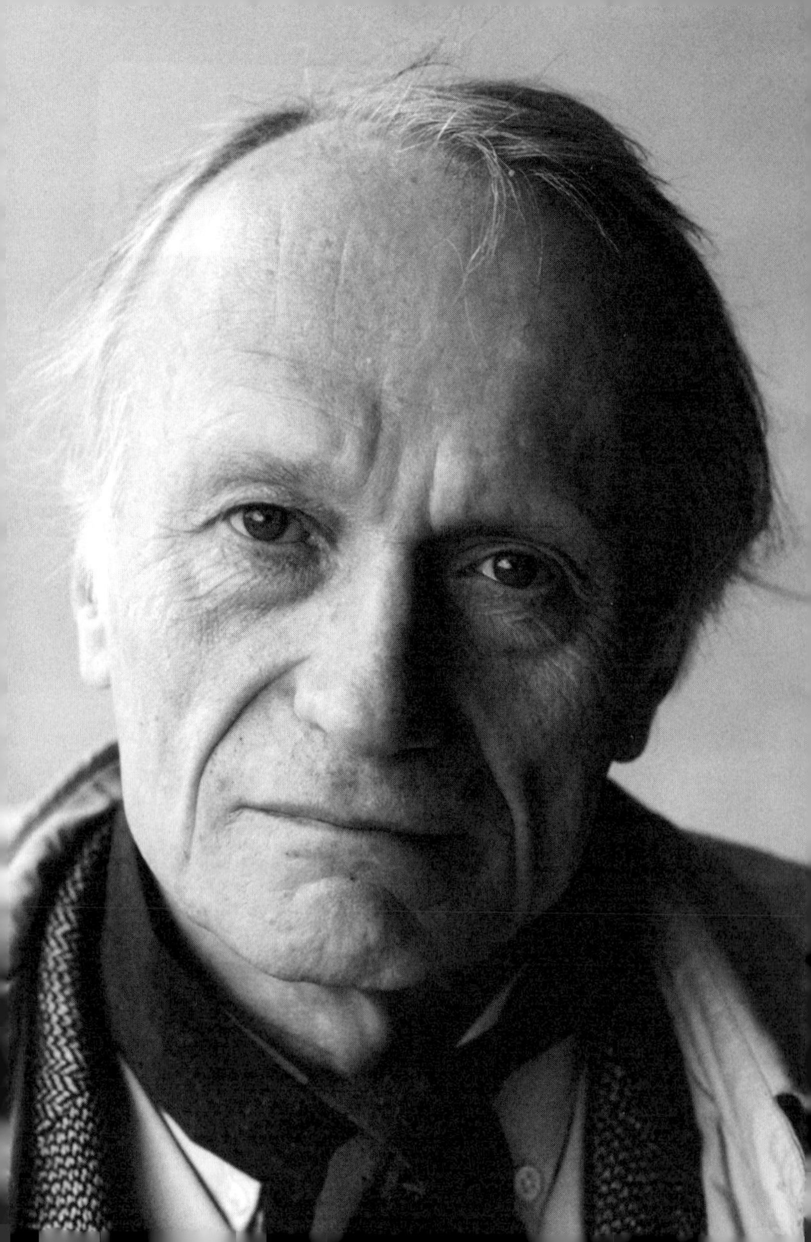

PETR KRÁL

LOVING VENICE

Translated from the French by
Christopher Moncrieff

PUSHKIN PRESS
LONDON

Loving Venice first published in French as
Aimer Venise in 1999

First published in 2011 by
Pushkin Press
71-75 Shelton Street,
London WC2H 9JQ

This edition first published in 2012

British Library Cataloguing in Publication Data:
A catalogue record for this book is available
from the British Library

ISBN 978 1 908968 85 2

Set in 11 on 14 Monotype Baskerville by Tetragon
Proudly printed and bound in Great Britain by TJ International, Padstow, Cornwall on
Munken Premium White 90gsm

This book is supported by the French Ministry of Foreign Affairs,
as part of the Burgess programme run by the Cultural Department of the French Embassy in
London.

www.pushkinpress.com

LOVING VENICE

VENICE, A PEARL OF A CITY that Kazimierz Brandys, reading from a map in the mind, locates with great precision at the "easternmost extremity" of our memory, is clearly also a city of extremes, not least in the feelings that she arouses. If she casts such a spell over her devotees, among them myself, that they are driven to despair like hopeless lovers, with others she comes up against an unswerving and sometimes openly violent rebuff. Her beauty, which resembles an artwork of such exorbitant and all-embracing delicacy that permeates every facet of the entire oeuvre, is such that it can cause even the most delightful lips to curl in disdain. A woman I know, herself as glittering and finely wrought as the work of a master goldsmith, coolly spurns the city's attractions as if fearful of being taken over by them—of being reduced to the size of a single jewel or a toy in its box. But, whether we go to great lengths to avoid her, or keep coming back like an addict to his drug (indifference appears not to be an option), what is certain is that Venice is an exceptionally closed—and enclosing—city.

Gathered together, as if crystalline for all eternity, even the depths of its cracks and crevices harmonious and inviolable, from the outset this urban labyrinth is reduced to its very essence—but such a process of concentration comes at a price. While the sparser, more sundry treasures of other cities prompt us to trace our own private path around them, in harmony with the tempo of our life and breath, our search for a way in or a secret hiding place, Venice leaves little room for manoeuvre; we move back and forth between its alleyways and *campi* as if we were pieces in a board game whose strict rules always send us back to where we started from—ourselves. When we come out of the station there is little choice but to go left, on one of the boats that sail along the Grand Canal and through the Rialto to San Marco, or to board one that takes the less obvious route to the right, along the Rio Nuovo—but whether we reach the Piazza San Marco from the Rialto by way of the bustling Mercerie, or from the Accademia, having walked over the bridge to the old marketplace after wandering through peaceful working districts, we are still on the same axis, following one of several alternative directions that flow with the same current. Not for nothing do signposts on street corners often point to the same place but in opposite directions—in the labyrinth there is no such thing as choice. ("On the map," writes Joseph Brodsky, "the city looks like two grilled fish on a plate; there is no north, south, east or west; the only possible direction is across.") To wander here is to keep retracing our steps, heading down alleyways where the only sound is that of our disarray, until, with an abrupt rattling sound as the shops close their metal shutters at twilight, they empty of any sign of life except the relentless pounding of our footsteps; in short, we soon realise that we are going round in circles on the back roads of our mind.

To find the fresh air of open spaces again, we have to go back to the outskirts of the city and look out over the Zattere and the Fondamente Nuove towards the great expanse of water and the nearby islands—to the façades on La Giudecca, drifting like folded paper on the surface, the peace-loving fortress of San Michele with its rigging of stately cypress trees. And yet perhaps the only thing that we find stirring about the blue-grey of the sky here, the sea which flows in all directions beyond the marker buoys, is that it brings with it the echo of the whispering city that hovers behind us, the discreet and private frisson to which she immediately reduces all living creatures

... But now I am really just addressing her initiates, the only ones capable of picking up such a muted message and taking delight in it. For it has to be said that for the layman, the average tourist, Venice has very little to offer.

There are no picturesque areas to keep us amused—the people of Venice live quietly—no (or very few) theatres, nightclubs or entertainment in general, apart from those that take place routinely during Carnival or a Biennale. The only cinema—to my knowledge—whose icy-cold foyer shines as brightly as a mortuary on the corner of a dark, gloomy alley near the Accademia every night, seems doomed to remain empty, and people merely hurry past it in their flight from the last few shops that are open—among them a glittering confectioners—or to the cosy privacy of a good restaurant beside a small canal which is known only to its few connoisseurs. Restaurants close early in Venice, in the same way that access to the churches and museums is strictly rationed, which tends to reduce visitors to little more than figures of anxiety amid the silence of the town—obscure, faltering silhouettes intent on not being late and going where their guidebooks tell them, only attracting attention with the odd, unobtrusive sigh before vanishing at the end of an alleyway or a bend in a canal, completely engrossed in their mission.

The initiate, however, is only too delighted when everyone else has withdrawn, intimidated, leaving the delights of the city untouched for him alone. There is no doubt that in high season the tourists manage to bury these same charms simply by being here, so much so that as a result of the constant jostling by the dense crowd in whose midst Venice finds herself, for a brief moment they manage to transform her into the gaudy image they have of her—and yet the sparkle and splendour that they see all around them, if they but look at the scenery, is no more than a view from a picture postcard, the hustle and bustle of some fabled festival in which the city seems to have immersed herself, but which is actually attributable to all the other modern-day extras carrying cameras just like theirs and wearing identical shorts and T-shirts. At these times Venice only reveals her surface beauty, her Canaletto quality—a selection of vistas and architectural styles, the splendour and sculpted harmonies of palaces displaying their cornices, pillars and friezes in the sunlight with the smile of a proud, self-confident truth allowing people to admire its sumptuous details.

Of the two painters who devoted themselves to extolling the city's virtues, only one of them really succeeded in capturing her depths—the true Venice, the secret, inner one never appears to us until she wells up through the silky lustre of Canaletto's *vedute* and becomes one of Guardi's uneasy views. Standing on the Piazza San Marco, we only have to glance up at the afternoon sky beyond the roofs, which a moment ago we thought was still quite glorious, to find its blue now discoloured into a dull, leaden tone—subtle yet immutable—which makes us lower our eyes as if we have just heard a judge pass sentence; all around, meanwhile, the palaces reveal the cracks in their façades, and their contours, along with the restless shadows—including our own—which are shifting around on them begin to flutter—to quiver in the same way in which, with a stroke of the brush, Guardi injects his scenes of revelry with an air of foreboding for the coming flood. At this very moment, night, which is poised to fall like a guillotine blade, seems the only fact that the day has to offer, while with an inner trembling the city reveals the layer of grisaille that lies beneath her surface and which is her true colour, despite all displays of splendour and surface gloss.

This grey, shivery, flaky Venice, which with her lack of entertainment is so inevitably tedious for the average visitor, now charms us with her candour alone, the unaffected way in which she shows us the essential things in life—how ephemeral everything is, how essentially ancient, and how any memories they might have are doomed to disappear. And, long before it fades completely, even the bright blue sky which lights up the rooftops above us recedes as if behind a sheet of glass, beneath the accumulated and intangible weight of time and the imprints it leaves on everything, most of all our personal vision of the world; the delicacy of the shapes and colours, the subtle variations of the textures which can be traced along the façades of the buildings, the precariously perched roofs, their chimney pots and turrets tilting hither and thither as if leaning on each other for support, the flimsy miracle of this precise moment in time which they bear up in their hands, that pristine—and very Italian—acuity with which we perceive them affects us too, through the collective memory, the centuries of paint applied layer by layer until they are no longer visible to the naked eye, and the resulting sense of plasticity with which they endow it.

So while everyone else seems to be submitting themselves—as we just stand and watch—to the ceaseless shimmer of the city, where other, more distant figures keep appearing beneath the surface of her latest performance, these amassed riches instinctively withdraw into the background, once more taking on the fugitive quality of simple whisperings to which everything is ultimately reduced. Beneath this outward splendour and variety we discover the prosaic poverty of all things, what Émile Henriot calls their "eternal frailty", which has no more dainty dishes to offer except this one last treasure—the diminutive subtleties of the grisaille. And if the city's alleyways suddenly empty at nightfall, if their activity ceases at the first metallic clatter of shutters closing, giving way to dusk and the drawn-out echoes that a life of seclusion casts over her embankments, it is because it is possible to see Venice herself as a hallucination which soon vanishes.

It is at this point that we feel a yearning for the things that slip away from us, especially those whose passing is inevitable. For although, thanks to its state of seclusion, the city gives the impression of maintaining the original world order as a last resort for a human race preoccupied with its own interests, she only reveals it to us when it is too late, as we stand weeping at its bedside as it lays dying, and which in a sense prompts us to confront our own mortality. Almost every moment we spend here seems to be over before it has even started, a victory that is impossible to achieve but which allows us brief glimpses of itself, although it is for ever beyond our grasp; the dream-like stage set which

Venice sets up around us is not designed for living in, the waves that rear up in the lagoon, brushing aside the glittering jewel-box palaces, conceal their beauty from us by declaring it to be under sentence of death.

Despite this, however, the observant visitor is not left dispossessed; the hesitant mist into which the city's gaze dissolves allows him, providing he acquiesces, to breathe deeply and evenly like never before. By embracing the drifting grisaille, by following on the heels of its merest inner conjunctions, he suddenly realises he is on the right path, and sets off along it all the more wholeheartedly for knowing that he is swimming naked in his own slipstream. (There are hidden recesses of Venice that are so empty that we could go there without any clothes on and not be seen.) While walking across an empty square which blazes white-hot in the sun, to simply notice the glow of the little black '*toscanello*' that we have just finished smoking, its brilliance suddenly solid between our fingers as if the pallor of the city has transformed it into a piece of metal, and then to think back to another square, where, outside a café, the blue-grey stockings of an unknown woman glowed in the same subdued way—this is all it takes to make us feel that we have moved one of our pawns forward a square.

We take just as deep a breath when we walk under the tall vaulted archway of the Church of the Salute and find that the interior is the same shade of grey as the impressive dome we saw outside (the "rock in mid-air" according to Robert Marteau); without even pausing, the mystery makes the pathway that has led us to it along nameless streets and embankments even longer, and simply moving from one place to its opposite side permits us to enter without having to make a detour through purgatory. (When we sail along the canals in a vaporetto, the faint glow that we catch sight of in the depths of a palace through an open window could just as easily be coming from some hidden mirror as from an opening in the wall through which the darkened interior breathes in the daylight; at night, the most lavishly lit windows, draped with strings of glass beads visible from outside, are similarly just gashes in the dense, dispassionate weave of night that stretches taut all around them.) In the same artless way, squares whose boundaries are marked out in sweeping gestures, either curved or straight, by pieces of grey marble on the floor of the church, continue the format of the game whose schema can be seen in the layout of the cobblestones on the squares and pavements; without even coming to mass we can still respect the sanctity of the surroundings by joining the other visitors in quietly pacing round the circle drawn in the centre of the nave by marble sculptures, or diffidently wandering round the edge, gazing at the void above and feeling the touch of an age-old sigh in the small of our back, along with the insouciant breeze. In a vain attempt to make this sigh last longer, as we leave we take hold of the crimson velvet curtain which, like an artfully pleated skirt, hangs in front of the great locked portal, and give it a gentle shake in the hope of wafting some fresh air into the shadow-light that lurks behind it, stirring up the intermingled eras and epochs that the church accumulates.

Returning another day, the liturgy that we encounter could hardly be described as importunate—in the middle of the circular nave, now enclosed by a ring of short posts with red rope strung between them, a lone cleaner kneeling in a shaft of dusty light prays for the assembled people as she quietly mops the marble. Another member of the congregation, which is hardly vast, is one of the city's secret, silent sleepers, leaning back in a chair, his gaping mouth lifted towards the dome above.

ULTIMATELY, THE CITY of the Doges only really enriches us by keeping its treasures in concert with the ebb and flow of a single, subdued medium; by allowing us to glimpse the harmony that quietly endures behind their opulent exterior, even if it means that our own silhouette is eventually absorbed into it. In Venice, the breath of the world is all the more exhilarating because it merely wafts past us, the dizziness we feel comes from the fact that every unique feature is engulfed up by the overall lack of individuality, like a variation on a theme that plays over and over again. The signs and symbols that the city continually lays before us, the gestures, impulses and beams of light which burst forth in a quivering mass with the spontaneity of an original idea—immediately creating a brand-new galaxy ready to start scheming and flirting—only exist to maintain the motionless reverberation which manages to reproduce itself by starting afresh each time. Every gondola that appears from under a bridge with its cargo of mineralized bodies—as if about to make their final journey—its whisper barely ruffling the surface of the water, is merely imitating the motion of the one that came before (in an identical scene of 'a passing boat'), while the lengthening shadows in the maze of twilit streets send footsteps scurrying faster over the cobbles without once changing tempo. Everything in the city is destined to tread water, its trembling outline for ever hovering on the threshold of absence so the great frisson can be maintained: the leaves on the trees, the awnings of the shops, the washing hung out to dry over the canals and the shivering green plants on the balconies, the water that laps against the embankments and the wings of distant seagulls that launch themselves into the sky.

In the dance of the gondolas, bobbing up and down one by one against the backdrop of a distant church in silhouette, their prows bristling with blades and little black axes—and here I am thinking of the ones moored next to the Piazzetta facing San Giorgio—there exists an oft-reiterated threat which subsides as quickly as it appears, while in a vivid silver cascade the surf dissolves its doleful shapes time and time again. The real hero in the tragedy that Venice stages endlessly for herself might be the quiet man wearing an inconspicuous, rain-coloured overcoat who is calmly reading the paper while he waits for the vaporetto on a busy landing stage; despite the bouncing of the pier and the wind ruffling the pages, the top edge of the newspaper remains perfectly in line with the horizon, the man keeps his balance, and, surrounded by the rising tide, carries on as if sitting in a library, a mere witness to the wrathful elements. The very image of continuity, it goes way beyond any agony, any day of reckoning that has been placed indefinitely on hold, wherein lies the 'Venetian way', as much as its underlying appeal. (According to Jacques Cels, "In Venice, even the tragedies are based on temporary expedients.")

There is one place in Venice, however, which is always out of reach, protected from evil as much as from bad weather—the place where the city takes its dead, the mournful quarter of the Isola de San Michele. However dark the sky might be when we set sail, once we get beyond the murky waters of the lagoon and the noiseless, airlock-like gates of the cloisters by which one enters, the cemetery is waiting for us, bathed in gentle sunlight, the tranquillity of summer drifting among its tombs. Who wouldn't be happy to stop off for a while, despite the clouds that can be seen gathering above the far-off towers and steeples of the city—and even the disturbing influx of new tombs, which in ever-more serried ranks jostle behind the older ones, urging them to make more room. (The crosses on top are increasingly perfunctory, while, surging after them, the anonymous area of grass that stretches beyond the cemetery is gaining ground—while the latter's haughty silence brusquely shuts itself away in its enclosure, not far from Stravinsky's tomb, whose only tribute is a pile of grass cuttings rotting by the wall.) Eventually, of course, and before the sky has even had time to cloud over, the fickle water will come trickling back in to irrigate the pathways, but by the time that day comes the world will have ended.

But until then, the reminders of the threat that hangs over Venice allow us to see her as never before, giving us a chance to understand what it is she is saying. To experience the whole enchantment we have to witness a sudden thunderstorm that rips open the balmy September evening sky, to run for cover beneath an awning at the top of the Rialto and watch horrified as panic-stricken waiters on the embankment at the other end rush to pick up lamps that have been knocked over onto tablecloths, rescue nicely laid tables at which, only a second before, diners were looking forward to a piece of culinary heaven. All at once the tantalizing trinkets scatter to make way for providence, whose livery they willingly wear, a crack appears at the back of this jewellery case of a city, exposing the abyss on—and against—which she is built.

In the now silent, empty streets, amid growling thunder and flurries of shooshing rain, Venice soon returns to the state of subdued anxiety that she endured during the plague; the palaces beside the *campi* that we scamper across on our own are taking refuge in their blacked-out bulk, as if they have suddenly burnt down, while in the empty church where we briefly seek sanctuary before re-emerging into the amphitheatre of a large square, the only illumination is the wan glow of lightning lashing ominously against the windows behind the altar. As we set off along the edge of a small square under the watchful gaze of a lopsided and now shipwrecked bell tower, the sky has turned completely white, while in the distance a shivery peal of bells sounds the alert. By way of answer to this timely prompt, and against a background of fiendish tranquillity, the rain seems to echo louder, reaching into the depths of the capsized tower where we think we now hear voices, screams rising up from the whispering water as if a camp full of travellers has been roused from sleep by the lightning's alarm signal. In our isolation we feel an immediate bond with an entire unknown community who seem to have been washed up by the shipwreck of time, their murmurings now brought to us by the Venetian frisson, and yet they might just be people who came before us, the living souls of yesterday who remain for ever nameless. It is as if these cries, in which they live on, whether because of the bell tower or some miracle, come to us from deep down inside ourselves, reverberating with the polyphony peculiar to the laughter, sighs and curses that are the stuff of everyday life, here encapsulated into a precious possession. And then, beyond the intertwining raindrops and voices, we catch the scent of freshly laundered sheets, which strengthens the weave by reminding us of the feel of fine, heavy bed linen, something which is known the world over …

Eventually we even start to enjoy the celebrated *aqua alta*, the floods that regularly inundate Venice between October and March. Like everyone else we have tried to avoid them, delighted to have escaped whenever we see the footbridge-cluttered streets in a city now dry and resplendent once more, which tells us that we have narrowly missed high tide; like other people we shudder at the sight of elderly Venetians, who, going out for their morning walk, inspect the manhole outside their front door and declare in a subdued tone that the water level is rising. The biblical downpour that greeted us on the morning after we arrived for our first stay here with D, however, came as a relief. For all the floods it caused, the rain, which began to echo in the little courtyard of our hotel just after midnight, soon joined by the muffled ringing of alarm bells, wasn't just in keeping with the period in question and the doleful delights of autumn—which that particular year were heralded by the muted colours—greys and blacks—of the fabrics on display in the shop windows; the torrential rain also creates a closer bond between us and other visitors, who like ourselves have to make unexpected efforts to value the city, and the greater the pitfalls, the greater our alertness and sense of independence as we roam the streets.

Confronted with this danger, the city on the waves is also more conscious of herself, her vocation in the midst of the flood tide. Tiepolo's paintings have twice as much power and grace in a Ca'Rezzonico whose foundations we feel shaking under the onslaught of the waves, and which we only reach after braving a succession of landing stages. When, returning late at night from one of our lengthy promenades, we shelter from the rain in a bar on the corner of a street now transformed into a canal, still open and blazing with light as if it were the last lighthouse in the world, the bodies of the locals who we join at the bar create a flood barrier with our own, soaked and chilled to the bone yet at one with the same foul weather it dares to defy (and which is visible through our raincoats, that resemble a collection of damp, ancient sheets). As we leave the bar, we set off to have a look at the nearby Piazza San Marco, now under water—but get no further than the entrance to the arcade that runs beside it, and yet, through a narrow porch, the Piazza is very much there, transformed into a tranquil lake in the middle of which, in splendid isolation—crowned by a tarpaulin but with the lights still blazing—stands the bandstand of the Café Florian. To our surprise the musicians are still there, and then suddenly, in the midst of the downpour they strike up a last waltz; we listen, filled with wonder, then applaud this noble serenade which doesn't seem to be for anyone's benefit, simply a challenge to the still and silent night. At that very moment, desultory applause not unlike our own comes from across the Piazza, where other nightbirds have obviously stopped in passing. Although we can't see them, we are all witnessing the Venetian spectacle par excellence—a collective tribute which expresses gratitude, not only to the spectral musicians who defy the downpour with the same panache as their counterparts on the *Titanic*, but to the city herself, for showing us how to go down in style, glass of champagne raised to the glowering sky.

If by simply setting out to be dazzled by a vast extravaganza we waste our opportunity with Venice, we nonetheless increase our chances of getting to know her the more we stop chasing after entertainment and immerse ourselves in daily life here. Although even the most ordinary gestures are probably doomed to failure—preventing us from the outset from becoming genuine residents—more than any other city, Her Serene Highness only makes herself fully available when we try, against the odds, to transform our visit into a stay, however fleeting. If we want her inimitable frisson to reach out and touch us from the depths of the grisaille, it isn't enough to just set off on a tour; we have to take our time, carefully select the right small hotel and settle in calmly and quietly, become acquainted with its tranquillity, with what goes on behind the green baize door, the same as anyone whose aim is to become part of the furniture, before heading back out into the street like every other normal citizen who isn't weighed down by thoughts of luggage or a departure date.

So we begin by strolling round the local area and its shops, to make sure that the city is really there, all around us in our isolation, less concerned about having a good time than with living our lives (what Claude Dourguin calls "one's ordinary eternity") against the backdrop of palatial scenery. Even if we are never quite sure when we arrive whether we are going to find that she has sunk beneath the waves for ever, in Venice we are overjoyed as in no other place on earth to see our favourite shop again, or the owners of a bar where we have become regulars, despite being faceless foreigners, and where diners are always served a delicious lunch with the same old gestures and remarks. And if some minor event should occur in honour of our homecoming, like in the wine merchant's hidden away on a corner behind the Tedeschi—the Post Office Palace—where the owner and his whole family suddenly assemble to greet a tall bearded man who walks in with a woman and a large dog, and, by way of greeting, joins in with the aria sung by a booming tenor on the radio—then what we have is as close at it gets to perfect happiness. Without sacrificing our anonymity, we feel among friends in a way we never have before, experiencing the same weather, breathing the same air as everyone else, whose slightest nod, beckoning hand or quip to the waiters we drink down eagerly, asking no more from them than that they continue their routine—introducing surreptitious little gestures of our own occasionally, holding a toothpick between our teeth to show that we too exist.

We feel the same soothing sensation of belonging when, on another occasion, we witness the quiet enjoyment with which a man casually sits down on his own among the fashionable crowd at Harry's Bar, a prelude to a supper that might be either a late or early breakfast. Despite his austere and very British elegance, the man—he is pale and quite elderly—appears to have come in slippers straight from home, where he has spent the day; the leisurely fastidiousness with which he chooses his food, only to ask for plain bouillon and two slices of ham, is patently that of a nearby resident and habitué who regards the opulent establishment as his local. We are aware that such informality is a priceless opportunity—even more so than the private income that probably creates it—that it represents the only acceptable way to live in the real Venice, and that we would benefit from becoming better acquainted with it by adopting this man's approach.

Waiting for us deep down in the fissures that we sometimes come across unexpectedly in the city is the secret of these humble gestures and events, whose purpose is to maintain the existing, noble order of things on the same scale at which, by their very simplicity, they manage to keep it alive. Among the city's greatest glories, at least nowadays, is her village-like tranquillity, the backdrop of stillness against which the slightest signs of life—sounds, gestures or words—retain their original significance. To let Venice under our skin, essentially all we need to know is that the bell boy at our hotel spends his nights playing cards at a club on the other side of town, on the same embankment where we have dinner, or to glance out of the door of the half-lit church where we are attending evening mass behind a row of wistful old ladies, and see the familiar sight of a chemist's illuminated sign winking at us through the first drops of the latest shower of rain. In a bar beside the little bridge that leads over to the Campo S S Giovanni e Paolo, everyone who comes in gets a drink from the bar and then carries it towards our table, staring at something in the distance—it is still raining, so they are keeping an eye on the water level in the canal, which can be seen through the window behind us; simply that. Yet we are grateful to them for embracing us so spontaneously with the camaraderie of their gaze, nameless bystanders though we may be.

We feel similarly indebted to the gondolier who suddenly stops with a boatload of passengers bound for the Riva degli Schiavoni, and casually goes up to an open window beside the canal, where, grinning from ear to ear, he is given a drink by the landlady, who is bustling about inside and treats him like a member of the family; plunging our gaze into the inn, which is on the corner of the canal and an alleyway, we are even more delighted when, through a window near where people are leaning on a small bar, we witness life backstage. Staring into the sink on the counter, we see a sparkling pile of spoons and screwed-up kitchen foil which has all the brilliance of a collection of precious silver … and so our gondolier, too, despite the part he plays in the show that Venice puts on for tourists, has helped us get a private glimpse of everyday life. For gondolas also venture backstage as much as possible, occasionally appearing from under a bridge in one of the quieter parts of town with just a pile of cabbages on board, or empty demijohns that clink against each other to warn people of their approach; early one morning, while wandering through the recesses of a palace where they have rented us a room, drawn onto the balcony by a muffled lapping noise, we see one carrying a single prosaic passenger, comfortably installed in the middle of the slim vessel, reading the newspaper. Between fares, some *gondolieri* have a quiet bite to eat on their boat, in the way other people go into the nearest church, sit in the pews and read the paper. (In their local bar, others leave the counter and sit at a table by the window, where they flick absent-mindedly through an open newspaper that someone has left behind.)

In the peace of the night, a passing gondolier singing with his passengers might be an expression of the city's romantic inner frisson; the brief gathering of passers-by who stand silently on a footbridge to watch them float past is the only custom that we are willing to take part in with other visitors. After the rest have moved on, we stay to watch a different group assembling on the next bridge along, and then leave them to go their separate ways as well, so we can be alone to watch and listen as the last lights, the final voices are swallowed up by the darkness at the end of the canal, inhaling them like the blackened trompe l'oeil background of an old oil painting. Scattered with diffident stars, the sky we see on the horizon, or above us between the palaces, takes on the faded tones of a dusty, centuries-old canvas of the vault of heaven, and then in unspoken collusion another lone stroller stops unexpectedly a few bridges down. It could be our secret double—who we have spent a lifetime searching for but who always remains hidden in the crowd—or perhaps it's just the old night owl from Harry's Bar? Before he goes on his way we give him a complicit wave, which in true dignified fashion he chooses not to notice …

Strangely enough, Venice has even managed to marry its modest charms with the recent invasion of mobile phones, despite their intrusive presence everywhere else on the planet. Whereas in a capital like Paris, where people flaunt themselves and their devices at every road junction or in the middle of busy streets, marching along blindly and yelling into the handset, Venetians seem willing to harmonize their calls with the everyday whisperings of where they happen to be. If, standing beside a canal, they take out their device with a certain pride—this is Italy after all—their conversations always include greetings for friends, giving the impression that these messages are just a subtle way of connecting two separate squares on the chessboard of this maze-like city, despite the fact that it is getting dark, shutting each of them off in their private isolation (most calls are made at dusk); it even seems that the phone companies position their masts with the layout of the area in mind, angling them towards spots with the most buildings and activity, in order to enhance the life of the neighbourhood. As they tend to be concentrated in places used by local inhabitants, their presence is preferable to that of the tourists who insist on roaming round these same residential districts.

After a brief outburst of evening animation, however, the friendly atmosphere of the ordinary working districts subsides back into peace and quiet, as if someone has politely but firmly cut the telephone wires. But before the night falls silent, there is still time for us to give ourselves a good hard shake in the midst of the great, living streams which come flooding through the twilight from all directions, bringing with them the myriad buzzings and hummings which mark the end of the daily grind, and in which, as if merging day with night, the last echoes of busy footsteps mingle with the first chink of glasses from the bistros. Once again, to experience this whirl to the point where it makes us giddy, we just have to pay a visit to the tiny little toilet in a popular bar we know, wedged in on the corner of an alleyway opposite a footbridge that spans the canal diagonally, and feel the heady effect of the wine as it comes rushing back to us on the night air, exaggerated by the sound of footsteps on the cobbles in the dark street outside.

The previous afternoon, on the Isola de la Giudecca, we had an intoxicating sense of what it is to be withdrawn from life, almost suffocated by the stillness and primitive atmosphere in this Venetian appendage. The few signs of activity that we managed to catch en passant did not only reveal themselves through telling yet subtle signs, but also, and with what seemed like greater urgency, in the diminished surroundings. Even the silence speaks volumes when, in an overgrown street lying prostrate beneath a lifeless sun, at the window of a small house we catch a glimpse of an unknown young woman lifting up the edge of a thin, green, lattice-like netting, which is there to keep us away as much as the mosquitoes. Further along, in an alley running off to one side, where all we see at first are the trembling shadows of washing hanging in front of a row of white houses, we are even more surprised at the sight of a jean-clad leg protruding from a doorway at the far end, its foot on a skateboard which it keeps flipping up and down almost automatically. During another visit a few years earlier, while standing outside a closed-down factory, it sent a shudder down our spine to hear the sound of an unseen typewriter coming from the depths of the dilapidated building, where someone was tapping away fiercely on the same key. The resemblance to the sound of a machine gun gave us the impression that what we were hearing was a tedious but insistent radio programme about the brutal sentences that are carried out in the mists of dawn every day, their ominous sound ringing out across barrack and prison courtyards all round the world. At the end of this same trip, when we went to see a stern, almost ecclesiastical building made of brick at the far end of the island—on the Mestre side—which had all the sangfroid of a haunted castle*, the sight of a man rowing in a nearby water channel beneath an overcast sky, and somehow managing to stay in the same spot among the reeds, seemed more like a messenger from that other forbidden zone—that time out of time, which, eternally suspended, prevents us from coming within sight of its tall, glassy walls, which are dulled by the soot of every twilight the world has seen.

Nonetheless, peripheral areas like La Giudecca still complement the city's distinctive charms. ("All that is left to us," as Claude Dourguin points out, "is to sail over to the island, make the mere little crossing, it has infinite appeal.") And if Venice likes to gaze into it as if into a misty mirror so as to admire herself from afar—or stare at her reflection and dream of being someone else—she actually belongs to the

* *The building is now apparently an uninspiring centre for artists.*

exuberant maze of streets on the main island. And yet silence still plays an important part in her life, as is illustrated by a discovery we make beside a canal, which is similar to and follows on seamlessly from how we viewed the shy young woman with the green mosquito net on La Giudecca—looking up from where the first drops of rain are darkening the cobbled embankment, our eyes meet the inexpressive face of an old woman leaning out of a window and solemnly hauling in the washing that is hanging against the front of the building, using the crook of her walking stick. The differences between the city's silences are no less marked for alternating with outbursts of a more frenetic life to which they are so inextricably linked that they derive their significance from them—and this is just to wax lyrical about the contrast between them and the crashing of the surf. The peace that reigns in the little local squares, and which rises to greet the sun among a newspaper stand, an elderly man leaning sedately on his stick and crates of vegetables laid out on the kerb outside a simple shop, only assumes its full significance when taken against the constant humming noise that we are vaguely aware of in the background, in the densely woven streets and houses where the city comes to recharge its communal batteries. For what makes an impression on us is undoubtedly the sense of community we find here, the bond that unites the inhabitants, dead as well as living—although it is inevitably a fellowship of passengers who will go down on the same ship.

At the same time, the routine maintenance that is carried out here lends Venice a somewhat bizarre air, more of a ghostly than a physical presence. Across the street from a high wall behind the Accademia, through a gap where we catch sight of an immaculate tennis court, are two grinning workmen who, though clad in the usual overalls, are clearly putting their time and effort into making cheeky remarks to people going past; even what they are doing, the older of the two stirring his brush round and round in a tin, while the younger one, who is more hyperactive, scrubs his brush up and down on the same patch of low wall, only serves as a form of ill-defined backing group to this male bravado. It is evening, when, outside a shop doorway, two other workmen are getting final instructions from a man who, rather oddly, is dressed like a sailor; without putting down the boards and sheets of glass that they are carrying, they are so eager to do the 'boss's' bidding that, accompanied by music from the shop next door, they perform a dance routine in the middle of the street.

If we want to steal one of the city's hidden secrets—even one of its treasures—whether a custom or a unique object in which we hope to find a concentrated version of its substance, then the best place to look is still the everyday life of the working districts. It is among the hurly-burly of the little bar opposite the diagonal bridge and its lunchtime crowd, with whom we are enjoying a dish of *nervetti*, that we suddenly meet with a gesture as unique as it is casual, as well as immediately *identifiable*—the way the barman abruptly withdraws his hand, which he is holding out to one of the waiters, and puts the coffee cup that the other has just passed to him onto the saucer. Whether he made it up on the spot, or whether it is a conjuring trick that he performs for his colleague after every meal, along with the laugh he gives, provides a brief insight into the private Venice and its noonday bustle. (By way of comparison, when we get back to Paris we encounter the French capital's own distinctive ethos in the not-dissimilar brio with which a waiter lines up the cups on the counter and then immediately turns all the handles in the same direction.) In a more personal sense, the inner life of the city reveals itself to us in the unusual sideshow that we come across one peaceful grey morning in the window of a shop selling caps in a secluded *campo*. Using a long thin pole fitted with what look like pincers, without leaving the cave-like back of the shop the elderly owner is gently shifting his wares around by means of this simple remote control … While every morning above the building next door, home to the great Party, just as gently they hang out a faded Red Flag, which has been wisely stored away for the night; the respectful lack of haste that the shopkeeper passes on to his caps also finds its way into the backstage corridors of the nearby hotels, where visiting couples, held captive by the siesta hour and low-season lethargy, sink into languid lovemaking as if hibernating for the winter.

Returning to the usual evening brouhaha beside a small canal not far from the Accademia—having completed a solitary stroller's daily chores—we feel amply rewarded by noticing that next door to a wine merchant's stands a fine old laundry. And as the sunset's last blush is fading, we can still summon up enough sparkle to give a silent accolade to a jogger who suddenly appears from a nearby alleyway, and by way of a last bouquet we flick the glittering stub of our *toscanello* against the antique greys and crimsons of a grand house on the corner. Comforted, we glance back at the vintners, where one of its customers is now paying tribute to us as well, holding aloft an upturned wine bottle.

As well as its unique and hidden mysteries, every city that makes a deep impression always prompts us to stay alert for some great discovery—a rite of passage which, in a flash, will reveal what lies ahead, a part of the world and of ourselves which is unknown to us. In Venice, too, inspirations of this kind are as personal as they are unremarkable, yet so submerged in her grisaille that it takes endless vigilance to be able to respond when they do appear. On this October morning, tepid and uninspiring beneath cloudy skies, I have nothing more in mind than a simple stroll in the gardens behind the church of San Giorgio, whose silhouette seems like an invitation when glimpsed from the opposite side of the Piazzetta. The keeper's polite but stubborn refusal to let me in is in itself unsurprising—although it alerts me to the existence of a powerful Organisation whose role is to safeguard this garden and places like it. Behind the man's façade, however, I sense the presence of a plea which is enough to change the course of events; instead of going away, I walk along the outside of the garden wall until I come to a place where I am able to climb over, only to find myself in an enormous building site, where a secret harbour full of motor boats occupies a part of this clandestine territory. I eventually manage to get to the far side and the garden proper, which slopes down gently to the lagoon. Once there I sit at the water's edge, suddenly finding myself completely alone, and equally surprised to hear—through that faint, scented, iridescent mist which Venice continually wafts and whirls around her periphery—dozens of clear yet disembodied voices coming from all directions, as if people are crying out to me from the day that is going on all around. These messages from every corner of the city, which carry in their wake the echoes of far-off building sites, the sound of hammers or engines running, seem to converge here in the depths of the stillness, revealing their polyphony in all its abundance …

But this is merely a prologue to the silent scene that I come across a moment later in the most secluded part of the gardens. In an overgrown amphitheatre, where, penetrated by its air of tranquillity, I quickly sit down, a stage as uncluttered as it is imposing seems to be awaiting the start of some private performance;

all alone in the middle of its empty boards, which are gently soaking up the pale morning light, stand the large wooden side pieces of the carved, rigorously angular and very Cubist trapdoor, discoloured and disintegrating with age. I am clearly in the presence of a minimalist theatre, particularly since I have had to come such a long way backstage to find it. Although the performance is inextricably mingled with a sense of absence in a way I have never witnessed before, the paradox of the empty stage conjured up by Rilke—whose lines come back to me immediately—is right here in front of me, as clear as a wellspring—in that essential silence in which every tragedy exists, both in embryo and as something that belongs in the past, appearing on the surface and then dissolving into itself again in the self-same impulse. An absence which, in the way it asks us to open our minds, also reminds us of a hidden source of hope ... With hindsight, my feelings of gratitude extend to the keeper's unbending attitude, which I now realise has allowed me to make progress—to find my own private doorway to the inner world without which there can be no revelations.

In the Palazzo degli Orfei, where the day before I had gone to pay a call on Fortuny, who lived there for many years (and which is now a museum dedicated to him), aside from the artist's work I tried to find something of the flavour of old drawing rooms and times gone by. As I get to the last room, however, having walked through others strewn with trinkets, luxurious fabrics and sumptuous paintings made up of a mass of coloured streaks and tatters, I have a sudden fit of giddiness; for, in the far corner of the room, where a sudden shaft of sunlight streams in through the varicoloured screen of the windows, it is as if I am plunging into the great man's paintings themselves, caught up in a web of brightly coloured splashes and splinters which, on a grander scale, are perfect renderings of the essence of his work.* Spattering me with paint, cluttering my path with furniture in this hidden recess, which is full of ungainly worldly goods—an old washbasin, a cast-iron goat's head and a red fire extinguisher—this radiant sheath of light is all the more unsettling in that it reminds me of a cage, which by its very touch makes living beings lighter while closing on them like a gentle trap. Ought I to have yielded to its embrace and stayed where I was, covered with brightly coloured, livid weals, and let my life's blood

* *They are actually by Fortuny y Marsal, the father of the famous decorator and former owner of the palace; a fact that makes no difference to the meaning of what is written here, however.*

slowly drain away into the basin? But, with one last and fitting sigh, I screw up my ticket and jam it into the plughole.

EVEN IN THE DEPTHS of her private, inner frisson, Venice is still open to the world's great perspectives, enticing them into her secret recesses and borne along by the touch of their breath. As we come out of San Giorgio and take a boat back into town, we get an international newsflash the moment we see the palaces opposite begin to reel, as does the declining afternoon, against the backdrop of daylight that still hovers over the horizon of the lagoon. Nothing is ever truly far away, History Past and Present, as much as their age-old foundations, continually appear and reappear in the daily changing scenery and the pure, simple elements of which it consists: the now brightly lit, now dark and sombre brick façades, the shivering tablecloths and awnings outside the cafés, the light that flows like a running stitch along the edge of the roofs and embankments. And, during siesta, all Venice can be found in the crumpled, rustling shadow that a church tower spreads across the folds of the canvas cover of the boat at its feet ("made fast to the paving of the bank, more way-worn than the sole of a marble shoe, a sunlit boat is where the infant melancholy lays his head"—André Suarès). All the hidden knowledge for which the city acts as a great repository reveals itself to us when the pallid façade of the Church of San Moisè suddenly unrolls its parchment in the dusk. This surface alone, a place where scowl-faced statues merge with the many cracks and blemishes, amounts to a message in itself, speaks to something deep inside us, and without recourse to formal learning, with its tremulous evening presence. In the same way, during mass in San Giorgio, everything is expressed by the priest's surplice, which suddenly shines out green beside the altar on the wave of light that has been so long in coming and on which, at the same time, everything and everyone that is left outside flows back into the church with a great sigh …

Seen against the background of these minor cracks that serve to continually distract Venice's distinctive shapes, colours and substance from themselves, the latter, which maintain their subtle poise and refinement as much as their deliberate reticence, whose ceaseless frisson creates a link between them and ourselves, are enough to ensure that we understand what the city has to teach us. In the minute perfection that their contours have acquired through time's erosions—as if sunken in on themselves—ancient gateways and statues, like those among the dusty folds of crimson drapes that the centuries have paled, and which hang ossified in all their opulent, immortal variety at the windows of the Procuratie—as if Venice's very charm has become a large, weighty object—in the russets and subtle greys of a façade with a mouldy, olive-green dado rail over which a tiny feather pattern is brushed lightly from top to bottom—everywhere a single, unchanging consciousness prevails like a drawing that is at once complete and yet vital, and which contains within itself a single pearl—the city's inimitable pallor. Everything is both ancient and modern, its die already cast, sketched out boldly across the limpid air of the here and now. Beside the Campo Santo Stefano one evening just before dinner, a young man stands on a pile of wet clay and briefly freezes like a statue while his friends rip the telephone receiver out of a nearby call box. Before I can catch up with him he is back with the group of laughing youngsters; returning a moment later, I see him outside the phone box, but now he only has one foot on the clay, and is casually tying his shoelaces. Even in Venice all the statues move, every figure is unfinished and somehow absent.

Although her memory is quite good, the city is a form of construction site where the world comes to work on itself and recuperate. On the wall at the corner of the Campo Santa Agnese behind the Accademia, ordinary holes filled with reddish dust have merged into the contours of the time-ravaged brick, and yet in front of another part of the wall, which faces the square, there is a pile of shiny new metal cramp irons. Near the middle of the square, slabs of concrete that have recently been lifted stand in the drizzle like grey blocks of ice, lined up ready for anything.

On a square at the far end of which stands the little church of Santa Maria dei Miracoli, washed up like a mythical ship, we are suddenly thrust into the world of modern democracy at its most rudimentary—a frenzied confluence of people and destinies, instanced in this case by a brief clash between a tourist who is trying to find her way, my own feverish silence and a cantankerous old tramp who is sitting on a bench and scaring the square's pigeon population by banging his stick on the back of the seat. Among all the comings and goings, the only way of making a connection between these disparate and unrelated elements which springs to mind is purely theoretical—such as the juxtaposition between the de luxe confectioner's beside the square and the chocolate box which the Church of Miracles—with its ivory and pearl-grey facings inlaid with dark-green or crimson medallions—reminds us of.

The grey of Venice has never quite soaked up the colours or the silver light, which, with the winged and agile feet of its watery whisperings, it constantly transforms into iridescent pearls, in the way ashes preserve the memory of a fire in their glimmering. When studied closely, the treasures that have been reduced to shades of the grisaille appear free of constraint, while in the seemingly regular black-and-white pattern of the marble floors in the churches there appear tiny, reddish-brown, crimson or pale-green fragments, like constellations of sparkling new beads, which, when viewed through glasses, enhance the uneven surface of the city walls that we come across on an embankment. ("The canal wears a coat of eye-like markings, yellow, red and green—a tiger skin in shadow, strips of orange peel and slices of tomato drifting on the shimmering ink surface of the water"—André Suarès.) Venice is certainly full of surprises; her box of tricks never seems empty. At a dull moment on a peaceful morning on the Zattere, alone with one or two cats and a few pensioners, we are suddenly reminded of the variety that exists in the world when, emerging one after another into the daylight from what is almost just a shadow between two walls, comes a little rich boy in his urban sailor suit, a cap straight out of a story book on his head—he isn't even seven years old—followed by his governess and, bringing up the rear, an elderly tutor in a gabardine raincoat, who, suddenly confronted with the sunlight, takes off his glasses and greets the great fiery ball with a scowl. Knowing smile or cynical snarl? We will probably never know. On the bank, meanwhile, a smartly dressed man has rolled up his trousers to show off his calves to some young women walking by, who, with their deep, voluted sleeves which ripple in the breeze, are giving nothing away, seagulls strut up and down blatantly on the rigging of nearby boats, trying to startle the unblemished bright-blue sky which is stretched out above the fronts of the houses on La Giudecca. As for the white-haired old man who has been kicking a discarded cigarette lighter around for most of the morning and has now skilfully managed to get it to land between a young woman's legs, he is apologising to her with a worried look. Not far away in a quiet little marketplace, an old woman starts cooing timidly, just like the pigeons who shamelessly descended on her the moment she opened the large, shiny tin she is carrying and tried to give them some seed, and which now fly off with a flapping of wings and a whistling of beaks and abandon her; beside the square, a moustachioed man in an immaculate suit contemplates the scene with the tranquillity of someone who has just emerged invigorated from his hairdresser, a folded newspaper under his arm by way of a shotgun. And, of course, we scrutinize him too.

When we come to the no-man's land north of the Grand Canal, districts that we have to pass through on the way to the Fondamente and the landing stage where the boat leaves for the Isola de San Michele, the view we have of them in the distance from the top of a bridge is often no more than that of a silent, stone-filled desert stretched out in the afternoon, with nothing to catch the eye except two lovers standing motionless at the far end, and we can't deny that this desert is enough in itself. And yet clandestine apparitions sometimes bob around on it like human marker buoys, each one more striking than the last. Just up ahead, beside a canal leading north from the area of Santa Maria dei Miracoli, a man is leaning against an ancient brick wall, standing on tiptoe as if to see how tall he is in comparison; we are even more surprised when a little fellow with a beard appears at the far end of the street, closely followed by a friendly faced giant, forming what looks like a circus double act. Just before they walk past, Hercules suddenly grabs the end of the midget's beard and gives it a surreptitious tug ...

On the evening when, together with D, we slip into one of the niches in the well-known café in the arcade, our choice of the cocktail hour luckily proves to be one of their quiet times. Yet once we are settled in the ancient, tapestry-hung alcove, at one of the swivelling marble tables that allow plumper clientele to get in and out, or smokers to politely pass requisites—ash-trays or lighters—to each other, we realise that others are enjoying the cosy surroundings too. Ensconced in isolated recesses, two unknown couples find themselves as much in the presence of our life stories, each with its own unfamiliar narrative and milieu, as we are in theirs, both equally part of the same vast eternal plan as are our individual destinies; if the woman at the far end of the room, whose elegance must be the product of extremely old money, now has to content herself with reliving her memories with the gauche parvenu—he looks like a self-made man from the South of France—who used to be her gigolo, then the young drifter and his little shop assistant, who like us are sitting by the window—although on the other side of the main door—are still only at the first, bashful stage, made even more timorous by a certain cavalier attitude that can be read in his gestures. And yet here we are, with our own love in full flight as well, once more submerged in that ever-changing current that is the novel of life, its many different voices audible beneath the clink of glasses as we toast each other's health.

Within the secret inner world of the Venetian maze, the strangest sights usually come in a cortège of others, even if they don't always appear at the same time. The apparition I encounter in broad daylight on the wide wooden bridge in front of the Accademia, a wild-eyed old sea dog waving a hideous bundle of twisted white electrical cables that looks like a clutch of vipers, is admittedly the one that makes the deepest impression, so much so that I think it might be the beast from the labyrinth, and yet the startling effect it produces can't be taken in isolation from the opening of a public event not far away on the festive-looking Campo San Barnaba, which, before bumping into him, I had left to run its course. Meanwhile, the first of the venerable old men were making their way up the steps onto a rickety platform that had been set up in front of the church, tottering along on their sticks and accompanied by a fanfare from some local girls wearing pillbox hats and impressive leather shoes, which the bright sunlight showed to be covered in minute creases … The woman who set up her easel on a deserted *campo* earlier, at the start of what is another cloudy afternoon, is likewise only a mirage, but, hanging from the top of some scaffolding behind her, at least an empty wheelbarrow is there to mutely witness her efforts.

BY ITS VERY AMBIVALENCE, Venice is an expression of the world in microcosm, nowhere more so than in the smell of her canals—disturbing and yet somehow ill-defined, much the same as its blue-grey and greenish tones, the scent of the stagnant water contents itself by sighing, enfolding the silt on its bed in a fond and velvety embrace. In the fairground-like attractions on the Zattere, to which, light-headed in the balm of early evening, we abandon ourselves, taking two paces back for every one we take forward, our desires just glide past each other like ships in the night. However much we rush around, view the light reflecting off the lagoon through special lenses that are on display at one of the stalls and flourish our overcoat like a torero's cape for the benefit of some women sitting on a stone seat, even put our glasses on to study the sapwood of a tree through a split in the bark, or fearlessly plunge our hand into a litter bin full of dead leaves and old scraps of paper, nothing will come of it—we always run aground in the shallows, as if the city won't allow herself to be eulogised except with a thorough examination, by going deep beneath the surface. And yet from the outset it is this, which by reducing our every attempt at conquest to a mere summary, brings our initial enthusiasm to its inevitable conclusion before it has even begun.

Besides, little things mean a lot in Venice, we only have to stumble slightly to set off unfathomable echoes. And the city undoubtedly misleads us, presenting us with vistas that exist only in our imagination. Trompe l'oeil is a much-used technique on this stage set, and until the last moment we believe that the images painted on a sign are real, while the palace gates in front of us seem to be drawn on the wall; on some of the bridges, strips of marble mark the edge of steps that are actually flat, as if they have sunk back into the cobblestones, while those on the landing stages lurk treacherously out of sight beneath a floating carpet of seaweed. ("A conglomerate of clay … clinging to grassy steps … how slowly … how splendidly is it dispatched into the void"—Jan Štolba.) On fine mornings the sun creates shimmering mirage-towns at the far end of shady streets—in the way the Calle Ca' Giustinian, next to the Piazza San Marco, suddenly draws our gaze to the banks of the Grand Canal—the *giardino* of a hotel nestling delightfully in a fold in the ground behind a lattice fence exudes the air of an overwrought and underemployed porter, imprisoning it for all eternity in an unlikely paradise no wider than a backstage corridor. And, in bright sunshine in the unpretentious gardens on La Giudecca, the enormous white funnel of an ocean liner looms up unexpectedly from behind the blossom-laden trees like a hallucination too perfect to be true; elsewhere in the labyrinth, beneath a bridge that we rush across in desperation, a white stone mask above a gateway similarly gives us a little nod, as if from the far-off depths of the night. In other places too, the city only seems to allow us to catch a glimpse so she can show us some private corner known only to her. Walking past a low wall on an embankment near the Zattere, when I stop to look over the gate, I see an oasis that I have known for years; a haven of tranquil greenery in the middle of which stand two or three pale and shivery chairs, a perfect replica of the small garden that appears in the work of an illustrious local photographer as representing the essence of Prague and the memories I have of it. Just inside the gate, like a form of seal, a dead leaf caught in a spider's web effectively shuts this place off from the here and now … Even while having dinner in an old tavern not far from the Rialto (Dà Madonna), a friend who mysteriously disappeared more than two years earlier suddenly walks in, and our eyes meet; yet although I hurry over to greet him, he slips away again as I am trying to negotiate a narrow pillar in the middle of the room. Rushing outside, all I see is an empty street in the pouring rain.

But sights like these are not mere illusions—far from it. Among Venice's constant back and forth between fact and fantasy, the truth sometimes stands out even more plainly; the passing of time has an unusually profound effect on this contracted urban landscape, with its eternal appeal of a simple sketch, where the elements batter relentlessly against the flimsy palaces that line the embankments like scenery from a puppet theatre. What is more, the way that the ubiquitous trompe l'oeil causes our eye to wander ultimately frustrates its attempts to deceive us, the squares on the chessboard of the labyrinth and the shimmering hallucinations which they take turns to create eventually dissolve into the limpid, collective translucence. All that remains is the whisper of brimming silver waves in the oval mirror opposite the Ca' d'Oro, or at a bend in the Grand Canal where the scenery moves aside to let the void come sailing through, like the ethereal blue which smiles at us from the large open gates behind the inner dock of the Arsenal. In the window of a bistro near the Scuola di Carpaccio, bottles that seem to hang in mid-air stand out like the definition of absence, merging their silence with that of the square outside as it absorbs the echo of a fading peal of bells.

In the midst of a pretentious ceremony that is reaching its height, the Piazza San Marco remains unmoved, merely an open space, reducing the ranks of war veterans in brilliant red uniforms who surround the square to a guard of honour for the lethargic company of pigeons. Barely stirring in the dusty white air, the birds are equally indifferent to any pageantry, eschewing the mid-air pirouettes that they might otherwise perform in an attempt to persuade the nearby statues to join them in what they call a dance. (Robert Marteau: "Flames which flicker in the sky, creating white statues to crown the Scuola San Marco. Slowly they turn, sway back and forth, then stumble … ")

If necessary, any performance in Venice will always stand aside in favour of a humble play of light and dark, sweeping away the extravagant stage set of ever-changing waves; a pool of light in the entrance to an alleyway which suddenly sets off the corner of a brick wall, a trickle of gold which coaxes a detail of a painting hidden in a nearby church out of the shadows, brings all this scenery within reach again, regardless of how it is apportioned between areas of varying significance. By even ironing out the differences between a palace and a maisonette, an Old Master and the work of an assiduous forger, the vagaries of light perpetuate a characteristic common among Venetians, in fact Italians in general; the equal regard they have for tacky baubles and a string of priceless pearls, mixing the two as the fancy takes them, doing the same with antiques and the latest gadgets, even in the most elegant boutiques tucked away in alcoves on the Rialto. As evening draws in, the old woman who owns a second-hand shop that stands almost below pavement level in a street near the Campo San Stefano has only one thing in mind—to fold the newspapers that she has spent all day reading, and then slowly and lovingly put them with the other treasures that are piled up around her on the shelves and tables of her Aladdin's cave. In the night ahead, whose coming this grotto eagerly awaits, we can be sure that these now-relegated pages will become as much a part of her riches as the scraps of exquisite fabric and antique photographs that she sells—at exorbitant prices—to her customers.

Before it gets completely dark, however, the city is anxious to show us its last few tricks, a disconsolate sun bowls along the rooftops of the Procuratie like an enormous red yo-yo, while, with a boom of its great bell, the Clock Tower vanishes into the mist along with its dull gold decoration; in a ballet without music, a roomful of trainee typists—one chewing a pencil, another tidying her hair—suddenly appear in a brightly lit window, where, along with the rest of the scenery, they must have been shifted, deceitfully and *in extremis*, from the hidden depths backstage. But in a balmy yet suddenly destitute breath of air which brings far-off cries from the marshes, the palaces now turn into strongholds made of some impenetrable, translucent substance in order to shut out the darkening blue of the sky, and as night sets in the only signs of life are some cheap luminous yo-yos (real ones this time), which stallholders near the Piazza San Marco are waving to help brighten up the darkness. Even our view seems restricted, the few glimpses we get are only of detached and distant realms—the top of the Doge's Palace, where among the pinnacles on the roof the bright light drifts from its moon-like salons as if in clouds of dust, while a pale-faced San Giorgio throws down a challenge to the far bank of the Grand Canal beyond the darkly creaking outlines of the gondolas and their licentious cancan. Closer at hand, we are now unable to make out anything except a few impersonal, curving folds glimmering above some posters shrouded in darkness on a nearby corner, even the sheet over the front of a building in one of the working neighbourhoods is just an expanse of hardened and virtually smooth plaster that stands across the street like an embargo. On a small veranda above it, a motionless old woman merges with the dark shapes of the plants that she has come out to water with a ladle full of shadows …

We have to face facts—we are not going to get any further, at least not tonight. Wherever we turn we find darkness, it is the only thing that makes us feel at home. All we can see is its façade, where the tall, bright flames of one or two lanterns reflect in a canal, near a small boat whose crumpled nickel seat glints in front of the dark, sombre curve of an arched bridge, whose reflection calmly traces a circle round it; beyond the bridge, the inverted image of a window suddenly lights up on the front of a building lost in shadow, its quivering and unreal blade of light barely scratching the watery surface of the night. This is what the theatre of life amounts to, a few uncluttered images—just black and white—which hold up the mirror of our solitude to us, the reflection of the window is simply a hazy screen onto which we project films in our mind's private cinema; all we can do is accept it, say nothing and just ponder on it, spare a kindred thought for distant friends who, in their own personal solitude somewhere on the other side of the night, are sitting quietly beside us.

Once we have found a room in a small hotel overlooking the canal at the end of the Accademia bridge next to the Piazza, it is true that we could go back and continue this tête-à-tête in another silent performance. Opposite, the magnificent Palazzo Cavalli-Franchetti, with the ancient red of its walls against which the rose designs and slender pillars of the windows—in the marvellous neo-Gothic style—stand out sharply with their brilliant white, is as unmoving as a timeless painting or era, oblivious to the to and fro of the sunlight sparkling on the surface of the oily water. As we settle into our little loggia that faces it, beside the great tide of watery power, it is tempting to let ourselves be borne away by this soothing sight and never return.

NONETHELESS, THE REAL SUBJECT of the picture remains in the background, where its twisted, creaking and unwieldy contours are always waiting to float to the surface, bringing with them the decay to which they are condemned. Seen through a rusty hole in a battered metal door on the far side of a *rio*, a pile of rain-soaked rubbish suddenly seems to express an absolute truth; the moment we touch the dazzling white earthenware guard rail of a bridge, we are literally shot through with cold, while the furnace of summer is rekindled in the stately, worm-eaten wooden door of a church in bright sunlight. Yet the city's ultimate treasure might be the anonymous heap that we come across on an embankment behind San Rocco, where at the last minute we decide to go for a stroll rather than visit the church and its well-known Scuola; outside an art gallery opposite an ancient stone house, where an elderly eccentric is attempting to hang some multicoloured toy windmills on his balcony, are the last remains of a fire, a pile of ashes complete with discarded items: old pens, a pair of worn-out shoes. After picking up a rusty nail and dropping it into one of the shoes, we are somehow reluctant to leave it …

The treasures of the churches and museums are not to be sniffed at; feeling our way in the silent shadow-light, the process of discovering them can become an act of initiation. This is precisely why we choose the darkest, most sombre churches, among which the high-stepping baroque decoration of San Salvador—near the Campo San Bartolomeo and its evening *corso*—is a veritable black pearl; we gladly lose ourselves in its dark inner depths, lit by unobtrusive, garnet-coloured vigil lamps in the shape of raindrops hanging from chains, while in the background, on dusty panelling behind the altar, the subdued red of a Tintoretto melts into the gentle light of an antique silver sky which hovers outside the window. Of course, a visit to any of Venice's historic buildings is inextricable from the panorama of everyday events, to gaze at her masterpieces is to wed their beauty with the activities and emotions around us. Carpaccio's paintings, in the grotto of his *Scuola*, seem to shine more than ever at the crystalline plashing sound of two elderly Venetians whispering to each other by the doorway, and a visit to the Scuola Grande di

San Rocco becomes a private ritual where we stroll beneath the great man's stormy ceilings carrying a small mirror, like a map showing us our path in life.

The high point of a brief visit to a small church, where on the way to the Island of the Dead we ask to see some frescos that are being restored, is a simple yet fascinating discovery that we make when a workman suddenly lowers an ordinary object down from the ceiling—a sort of wooden frame like a set square on the end of a rope that runs hard up against the wall in one corner, and beneath which he wedges the bottom of a long curtain and then hauls it up to the ceiling; simply that. With a movement of his hand, the frame—stretched along the pleated edge of the curtain as if holding the train of a long dress—rises up again, brushing against our fingers, and yet somehow we think we have touched the very soul of the church, its half-lit shadows, even come to a fuller understanding of its fine frescoes.

Another of the city's symbolic treasures, although less comforting, is the grotesque doll whose remains we find at the far end of an embankment among rubbish washed up at a bend in the canal. A dream we have about Venice could be summed up by an old tradition where residents have dinner while hanging out of the window; serving the meal on the window sill, and with their back turned to the street, they keep themselves in position by sticking their knife or fork into their plate. Yet the Venetian gem par excellence has the limpid qualities of an ordinary event—such as the bundle of white sheets tossed over an armchair in the lobby of my old hotel, washed with sunlight and the reflections of pale, opalescent raindrops on the windows. Alone in the depths of this dream-like labyrinth shines all the nakedness of the approaching day, and any splendour dissolves into the cool, fresh air that we now breathe.

ALTHOUGH OUR STAYS in Venice tend to be short, we always leave traces behind us. Every time we come back, a little more of our being threads its way into her tapestry, and so the memories of our visits gradually create a synopsis of our personal history. Each one appears in a different perspective, according to the friends who were with us, nearly all of them women who played an important part in our lives.

On the first trip, which was with V, at that stage still hitch-hiking and eager to see new sights, we decided to treat the city like an enormous living room, a vast nursery, in line with our youthful innocence and kindred spirits. Unaware that our arrival coincided with the end of the legendary Festival, we mingled artlessly with the distinguished guests in dinner jackets and long dresses in the evening streets and on darkened landing stages, shamelessly participating in their glamour along with our rucksacks, which were still spattered with dried mud. In the same way we tried to entice other people into the alternative, non-stop private party which we were determined to have, even if we collapsed from exhaustion in the process; one evening, we made up for our first bill at a café on the Piazza San Marco by collecting all the empty glasses that we could find on the pavement, and then persuaded the staff in a little bar next to the square to give us a non-stop supply of wine or brandy, which we spun round on a small chromium-plated tray between us as if playing all-night roulette, under the complicit gaze of the owner, who became more liberal with the drinks with every round. Later we indulged in reckless dance routines and mime acts, swaying from *rio* to *calle* like a pair of bemused epileptics, but, failing to elicit any response except raised eyebrows from a few passing tourists—the city was meanwhile going about its business—we commandeered a covered landing stage, settled into deckchairs surrounded by piles of comics and had a nice nocturnal siesta. The next morning, in full public view, we took it on ourselves to get even with the hapless pigeons on the Piazza, throwing them handfuls of corn mixed with coloured glass beads. Even if our feathered friends were indifferent, at least the square sparkled more beautifully than usual for the rest of the day.

The evening before we leave, on the same square, the strapping figure of a gondolier outside the door of a bar gives us an idea for one last act of bravado; pretending to want to find out if Venetians are ticklish, I walk up to the man and slide my hands down his ribs in a brief but firm *glissando*, and then go back to my girlfriend when I don't get any reaction. But I'm too hasty in my assumptions; with a laugh the man calls me back over, amused by my little prank which he says livens up his otherwise uneventful existence, and—no doubt equally enchanted by my companion—asks us to have a drink in the bar with him and one of his fellow boatmen. In no time at all the two men, now our guides, are giving us a final reward for our services by taking us on a grand tour, during which, graduating from acquaintances to friends and from parlour to kitchen table, we discover a whole new backstage Venice—which, as a result of the drink, soon becomes almost hallucinatory; when we finally decide that it's time to go, a sudden downpour completes our disarray—as well as cutting off our escape—by transforming every alleyway into a raging torrent. Even if we eventually manage to get back to the hotel, when we wake up the next morning we make an unsettling discovery—part of V's underwear has disappeared on the way back, somewhere between the last bar and our room. The hazy memory of some other hostelry—where, in a lurching dance, indecent but innocent, we tried to carry on the party all by ourselves—is not enough to put our minds at rest; it takes the old veranda where we sit one last time before leaving, as well as the bright, clear morning sky, to do that.

By shutting ourselves away on the outskirts of a working-class district after some overwhelming public festivities, in a reflection of our own tentative relationship, A and I have only limited contact with the city. During a windswept and freezing November, our silence is barely interrupted by the spontaneous aplomb with which the hotel receptionist absent-mindedly whistles a well-known aria as he writes our names in the register; in the chiaroscuro of our room, under the gaze of a reeling church tower that loiters outside the window, our embrace fades away to a sigh from a drop of champagne fizzing beside the bed.

As is only right, H and I begin our honeymoon under the auspices of Venus, staying in the biggest room in 'my' hotel near the Campo San Barnaba, where we sink into the heavy sheets—a loving firmness, at once cool, fresh and full of substance—as if into the embrace of the city's most motherly bed; one evening before we leave, we foolishly trust in a restaurant's fashionable reputation and end up by having a most un-Venetian experience—a bad meal. Afterwards, when I try to make up for it by angrily devouring the first hamburger I find, along with the lukewarm, insipid meat I think I can taste the universal insignificance of everything ... But between the two extremes of an unwelcoming restaurant and our friendly hotel, there is time for me to find a sunny alleyway, where, standing with my back to the light, for H's delectation I masquerade as a violinist; by way of a bow, I scrape away at the strings of my invisible instrument with the walking stick which I now always need to take when I go for a walk.

The small hotel where E and I stay, next to the main square, has a view over the canal—and the Isola di San Giorgio—all the way out to sea, but our room looks onto a small courtyard, beyond which, opposite our window, there exists a secret place that lives behind closed doors. The pediments and tiled roofs that fade into limpid, almost aqueous half-light every evening, the bells that sprinkle chimes over the flimsy aerials, are as modest as they are crystal-clear, while beneath their tender, tremulous and rather mere appearance lies a solid, granite-like structure; we sense we can rely on it, cling to it as if to a familiar base, we feel safe here in the depths of winter, even protected from the cold. In contrast, the screams of an unknown Amazon on the floor above, which come soaring across the courtyard one morning just before dawn to announce her climax, only emphasize the vast silence of the place.

In streets filled with twilight fervour, when we mingle with the passing crowds, somehow everything seems to be a diversion, objects stand out by their lack of similarity. On a hidden but lively embankment which we come across behind the scenes of San Marco, the dark stone buildings combine Gothic austerity with the sleek, functional simplicity of the black sign that is fixed to one of them, where the name 'ST-PAULY' stands out in white letters, like on the front of a railway station; the brightly lit rooms inside the open windows, which have the severe look of enormous caves, are brightened up by a vast collection of brilliant white lace, tablecloths and coverlets, either fringed or openwork, and which flutter as one in the breeze. On the steps of the bridge that leads to St-Pauly we are suddenly surrounded by a crowd of Japanese men in three-piece suits who come out of a building with fixed, unpleasant grins on their faces, as if they have just bought it. As we are glancing through the collection of lace in the next-door building, some more offspring of the Land of the Rising Sun, this time of philosophical bent, float past in a boat with a gondolier whose voice echoes off the front of a long building on the far side of the canal; going to the window, we are met by a silent barrage of flashbulbs which whiten the dark façade for a moment. The air of animation that exists here constantly creates connections between people and places, even nightfall no longer seems so inevitable.

Yet there seems to be something fundamental—a whole world—concentrated in the interplay of bright light and different textures, an urban core beneath the buildings that look onto the silk-like darkness of the canals, the stone walls and caverns zigzagged with white—whether lights or lines of washing—and the glossy jackets and dark glasses worn by foreign visitors parading in front of the pitted façades; a world which signals to us, shares its exuberance, although only in the way a film does, by projecting ghostly images onto a screen. In another part of town, as a gondola glides past with an ageing beau serenading in the bows, my young friend sums it all up when she sighs: "What a shame that everything comes to an end!"

So, here with you in the underwater city, we finally come face to face with the truth of life; not for nothing are the sombre shades of winter your favourites, for the love we share is also a tender and complicit acceptance of our own mortality. Is that why the loose—'morbid' in Italian—and elegant folds of your silk scarf, flecked with tiny black dots, blends so perfectly with the contours of the armchair where you briefly dropped it, or why we can sit opposite the Piazza San Marco on two chairs that have been left outside as if waiting for us? When we go back to the burnt-out theatre we don't even think of raking over the ashes, simply of having a last drink, and the hotel with the same name, although by now in darkness, is still friendly enough to open up an enormous public room for us, and leave us alone in the shadows with our drinks. We are surprised to rediscover the crisp fresh taste of fragolino, a wine with a strawberry bouquet that we know from a summer spent in Tuscany, and yet everything seems to stand to reason, as if the night herself is always mild for those who believe in her. Admittedly, when we come to pay for our drinks, the receptionist is surprised when we tell him that we aren't actually staying there, but he just laughs it off, and wishes us a safe journey through the empty streets, back to our own hotel.

NONETHELESS, WE DERIVE the most pleasure from our stay in Venice when we accept her for what she is, and disregard the various vulgar misconceptions that circulate about her. The best way to achieve this is not to entertain unreasonable hopes or ambitions, and to expect—and do—as little as possible. In this way the mere thought of being bored will never cross our mind, we will concentrate on what we are going to do, see and experience. We will put our efforts into wandering the streets and alleyways untiringly, our only guide the way they insist on rolling themselves into a ball, gliding past shops and boutiques without making any unwise purchases,* going into churches and coming straight out again, having inhaled their sweet smell; as we walk down the street we will hear the echoes of conversations

* *Despite the fact that—as Brodsky writes—"The very way in which the colouring and the tempo of the façades attempt to mellow the changing shapes and colours … of the waves can persuade us to pick up a scarf, a tie, anything vaguely stylish … "*

and radio programmes, without attempting to find out where they are coming from, we will go round in the revolving door of the palatial Hotel Danieli on the embankment, just to check that all the keys hanging on the wall behind the receptionist still have a red bobble attached to them. We will regard the city's charms as no more than signs and symbols that we reveal to ourselves, we will know how to accept the most attractive invitations without worrying about rival offers, without differentiating between the hotels and restaurants we frequent and those we avoid, between the food we sample from the—always tempting—plates on the next-door table, or between the unremarkable and yet, in our eyes, suddenly glorious paintings in a church filled with slanting sunlight and the masterpieces that are for ever hidden in the shadows; we will take care not to distinguish between the ancient palaces and the scaffolding and building sites that stand next to them, not to choose eternal beauty at the expense of the beauty which the city—in her profound compassion—bestows upon the most mundane everyday objects, we will be as appreciative of a grimy façade as we are of the elegant pink-and-pale-green doodles scrawled across the plastic canopy of the phone box in front of it,

—we will savour the brackish bouquet of ancient wooden doors and shutters as much as we do the seductive aroma of freshly roasted coffee, scented in the middle of a busy market square, we will pause, not only in front of pitted, decaying walls, but also outside the fortified entrances of grand residences (the little gold plaque bearing the single, succinct word 'CINZANO' beside a doorbell on the high wall that surrounds a building on the outskirts of the city at siesta time), to reflect on what we can learn from them,

—among the lush cornucopia of the old market, we will always be intrigued by the wriggling of countless tiny claws in a pile of shrimps, which move with the subtle yet persistent precision of the finest clock movement,

—we will inhale, quite impartially, the smell of washing hanging on a line in front of nondescript buildings beside a canal, we will flutter in the wind along with the humble garments (on a T-shirt, the two words 'THE WORLD' stand out like an impetuous demand), in time with the rhythmic pounding of the waves against the landing stages, the winking and blinking as they reflect on the front of buildings and the frantic dance of a white plastic bag flapping against a window in the wind,

—we will accept the price of the goods and services we are offered—even if they turn out to be too high or too low—just as much as we will the unsettling female visions, the dark radiance of a brunette in front of the pale, lacklustre bricks of the Campanile late one afternoon, or the understated inferno that smoulders beneath the surface of a young English face near the Bridge of Sighs at midday,

—we will never intrude on the golden twilight of the cats, world-weary queens stretched out in the sun on the Zattere and elsewhere in the city,

—we will be happy to flirt light-heartedly with the marble angels that stand sentry on the roofs, to dip our hand into a canal and then, while it is still wet, rest it on one of the rubber floats that are fastened to the bank to stop boats from bumping against the stone,

—we will gradually elevate ourselves by gazing at the graceful flowing curves of the canals and the ethereal shapes of the palaces planted beside them, beneath a milk-white sun whose pallor suddenly breaks through the frail curtain of mist,

—we will be as unsurprised to come across a porter balancing a crate on his head as we will to see a cluster of silhouettes blossom in an alleyway, for us it is all part of the secret existence of a pure, natural world that is renewed with each new day, and which includes a few random ghosts who fade as quickly as they appear (a gondolier standing on the prow of his boat who suddenly takes on the role of *orator*, an illusory drawing room glimpsed in an upstairs window where two empty armchairs sit side by side in solitary contemplation of a quietly flowing canal,

—and even the little girl who stands in the brightly lit entrance of a church as it is beginning to get dark, and squeezes her young mother against the door as if to just make her laugh …),

—we won't watch out for anything except the little incidents afforded by the twilight, the unhurried bustling of two men carrying a fridge across a bridge near the Zattere, the breath of air that soon slips away into the depths of night as a nearby shutter slams,

—we will find a fiery desert landscape in the dazzle of late afternoon snow scattered across the Piazza San Marco, tearing holes here and there in its unvarying grey, from the paving stones and weary pigeons to the façades of the buildings and venerable old awnings that stand beside it,

—we won't expect to see tightrope walkers on high wires stretched across the sky above the Piazza, although we think we catch sight of them every day at twilight, stepping nimbly over the lamps that are suspended from the wire, and which suddenly light up as if gently imploding,

—we won't be alarmed if we look up and find we are under surveillance by the pigeons that nest on the edge of the roofs or in gaps in the tiles,

—nor will we be terrified to wander off the beaten track in a shadowy and empty labyrinth after dark, into the furthermost uninhabited recesses where the only landmarks are statuettes of the Madonna hidden away in ill-lit alcoves, marble slabs with bewildering bas-reliefs inlaid with dust, low archways where a light bulb hangs inside a wire cage above it, shrouded by shadows that enclose it like a spider's web,

—we will never forget that wherever we go, the two of us will rarely be apart, that we will meet again in the house we share in the half-light of our flickering inner life,

—most of all, we won't be surprised to find that Venice actually exists,

—occasionally pausing at the brimming basins of the fountains on the *campi* to have a good long drink of water, finding in the blissful expressions of unknown couples the reflection of our own delight to be here, thinking of those we love and have loved,

—we will look for the city and keep on looking, by coming to see her, exploring her in the nakedness of even the most trivial event which immediately reveals her deepest depths to us, the simple blue-grey ribbon of an empty canal, its surface barely rippling, which we catch sight of beyond the arches of an embankment, beneath a pinkish façade which the water has dyed green at the base,

—we will notice that as they get on or off the vaporetto, passengers instinctively form a kind of funeral procession, sometimes solemnly headed by a suitably attired Michel Deguy,

—the morning before we leave, on a now-familiar embankment near the hotel, we will once more catch a faint breath of fragrance drifting from a hairdresser's doorway, and inhale it carefully, allowing it to mingle with the smells from the canal as well as those from a fishmonger's stall on the bank,

—and then finally we will be able to break the spell and leave Venice with no regrets, aware that if we stayed any longer we would founder by gazing too deeply into ourselves. We linger, but only briefly, in the canal-less streets between the Scuola San Rocco and the station, held back by their Sunday stillness and a vaguely watery sun, as if it wants to sit and dream and not have to hurry across the sky; trailing our suitcase as we walk past houses and gardens shut in by high walls, taking deep, deep breaths of fragrant air until we get down to the dregs and swallow a lungful of rotting dead leaves, we suddenly hear footsteps behind us, some people who have been to Sunday lunch with the family and are now going home, a few doors further down. At the same time, and despite ourselves, we overhear some of what an elderly but still robust father-in-law is saying to his more unassuming son-in-law, who with the assertiveness of the common people he is taking to task for this exact same shortcoming: "*Tu—troppo sottile, certo, certo!*"* At once poignant and reassuring in that they restore the humdrum to Venice's everyday existence, while at the same time, on the very banks of her deadly canals, proving how serenely this prosaic quality endures, in a sense these words come as a consolation; so when, a little further on, we glance in the window of a café and catch sight of a red ball speeding across a billiard table towards the railway station, we too stride out in the same direction.

Paris, Spring 1998

* "*You—too subtle, of course, of course!*"

ACCOMPLICES

Joseph Brodsky, *Aqua Alta* (Gallimard); Jacques Cels, *Journal de Venise* (Bruxelles, Le Courrier du Centre d'études poétiques n°176); Claude Dourguin, *La lumière des villes* (Champ Vallon); Émile Henriot, *Venise d'autrefois* (L'Illustration n° 4565); Robert Marteau, *Venise en miroir* (Calligrammes); Jan Štolba, *Le chien de Venise*, (Po&sie n° 84); André Suarès, *Voyage du Condottière* (Granit).

Pushkin Press

Pushkin Press was founded in 1997. Having first rediscovered European classics of the twentieth century, Pushkin now publishes novels, essays, memoirs, children's books, and everything from timeless classics to the urgent and contemporary.

This book is part of the Pushkin Collection of paperbacks, designed to be as satisfying as possible to hold and to enjoy. It is typeset in Monotype Baskerville, based on the transitional English serif typeface designed in the mid-eighteenth century by John Baskerville. It was litho-printed on Munken Premium White Paper and notch-bound by the independently owned printer TJ International in Padstow, Cornwall. The cover, with French flaps, was printed on Colorplan Pristine White paper. The paper and cover board are both acid-free and Forest Stewardship Council (FSC) certified.

Pushkin Press publishes the best writing from around the world—great stories, beautifully produced, to be read and read again.